*"Were I to await perfection
my book would never be finished."*

— Tai T'ung

"Amen"

— Bill O'Hearn

FROM THE
HEART
OF A CHILD
AND OTHER LESSONS
TO LIVE BY

Entheos Publishing Company
P.O. Box 970
Wilsonville, Oregon 97070

First printing, 1991
Second printing, 1991
Third printing, 1992

ISBN: 0-9626161-0-9

Library of Congress Catalog Card Number: 91-72584

DEDICATION

TO MY WIFE
GLORIA
FOR ALL THE YEARS OF
OUR LOVE AND OUR LIFE

AND TO
MY MOTHER
MARY O'HEARN FISH
WHO ALWAYS MADE ME FEEL SPECIAL

ACKNOWLEDGMENTS

There are so many close friends who have contributed to my life and therefore to this book that I could not possibly list them all here. However, I want them to know that they are an integral part of my thoughts and that I love them and thank them.

There are also those I wish to thank who have contributed time and energy. Among these are: Kathy Hove, for the hours of proofing, punctuation sleuthing, and thoughtful contributions; Alice Suyematsu for her time in transferring my MacIntosh disks; Julie Johnson for back-up support; Ken and Roberta Debono for so generously sharing their experience; Heather Kibbey of N.W. Publishers Consortium for encouraging me as to this book's possibilities; Thorn Bacon, my editor, for introducing me to the world of cutting and slashing, and for doing it with kindness; Ursula Bacon for backing up Thorn; and Richard Ferguson, a rare mixture of computer and artistic talent, for the cover design and formatting.

Special thanks go to: Judy Bailey for reading the original manuscript at least three times and believing I had even more to give; Barbara Egerman for reading and giving me her caring opinions; Don Egerman who from the beginning was a bastion of unwavering support, and believed that what I was doing had substance and meaning; Von Hansen for his encouragement, thoughts, and example of personal growth; Steve Newman for his constant support, insight, and example of heightened awareness; Tad Sweet for his willingness to nudge me when I had doubts; Roger Zener for his creative and helpful advice; Arthur Smith, Cliff Canucci, and Peter Suriano for their extra push; Don Eastburn for being a model of friendship and love; Greg Hansen for duty above and beyond as reader, encourager, friend, and dreamer; and especially Eveard Fish, my step-dad, whose example of gentleness toward people and things has had so great an influence in my life.

Additional thanks go to Dr. Lynda C. Falkenstein, her exceptional associate Suzanne Perkins, and the talented Candace

Swenson for their combined efforts in bringing this book to the marketplace.

Appreciation and gratitude go to Dr. Denis Waitley for his generous endorsement, and who, through his books and tapes, has been a role model for me and without whose personal encouragement in 1985 this book might not have been written.

Also, special thanks go to Lee Gedeiko, Dr. Waitley's personal assistant, for her spirit-lifting enthusiam for the message of this book.

And finally, extra special appreciation to Elizabeth for her encouragement, advice, love, and belief in me; Roger Asbahr, Mark Philip, and Mark Weir, my sons-in-law, for making it a pleasure to be a father-in-law; and to my children, Molly, Patti, Julie, and Chip, who make me the luckiest Dad on earth and are the inspiration for this book.

TABLE OF CONTENTS

INTRODUCTION

This is a book about life. This is also a book about love.

At one stage of our family life I felt the need to spend more quality time with our children, so I decided that each Friday night I would take one of our four out for dinner and some real one on one time, an "Evening with Dad." My idea was more brilliant than my follow through.

From the Heart of a Child is written to Molly, Patti, Julie, and Chip with love from Dad for those Friday nights we missed. Within these pages are lessons I would liked to have shared - had I been aware of them myself. The years have added to my experience and my perspective, yet I know the lessons are incomplete. They merely mark the trail I am on. My overall awareness is that the farther I go the farther I see.

This book is also written to you, the reader, with the hope that should you discover something meaningful in these pages, you will take the time to share with someone you love.

1

The Power to Choose

"Choice, not chance, determines human destiny."

— Anon

The Power to Choose

Choice has been described as the greatest gift we human beings have been given. Choice gives us the ability to create our own world. It allows us the opportunity to give meaning to our existence.

Many people, however, don't use this gift in a self-directed way. Instead of taking charge of their lives by making conscious, purposeful choices, they drift along letting circumstances dictate results. The net effect is that no choice becomes a choice.

This is living life by default, and those who operate in this mode are constantly bemoaning their fate. They blame everyone but themselves for who they are, what they are, and where they are. They assume the role of the victim. So let me make this point loud and clear. You are who you are - and you are what you are - and you are where you are by virtue of the choices you have made - whether by intent or by default.

That may be the bad news. The good news is that you have within you the power to change your life by taking charge of your choices.

Circumstances will not always be right. That is just the way things are. It is the choices you make in answer to those circumstances that determine your future.

I have had my fair share of adversity, and while I may have had no choice about the adversity, I absolutely had a choice about my response. I could have chosen to feel sorry for myself or I could have accepted the situation as an opportunity to grow. Regardless of which I chose, the distinction was clear. The choice was mine.

So why don't people take charge and make good choices? With many I suppose it is a matter of ignorance. They believe their personal history will never change. "This is the way it has always been and this is the way it will always be." With others it is a matter of apathy and with a few it is just plain laziness. For them it is easier to float than to constantly be bothered with resetting the course. It seems they would rather settle for a known misery than an unknown joy.

There are people in the world today who truly are victims of difficult circumstances, but even they have choices. Dr. Victor Frankl addresses this important point in his book, *Man's Search for Meaning.*

Dr. Frankl, a world renowned psychotherapist, recounts his years of horror in a German concentration camp. He discovered that his captors could control everything about him except his mind. Dr. Frankl concluded that those who survived the death camps had made a conscious decision to live. Those who died chose to give up.

Most of us will never have to face anything as devastating as a concentration camp. But if we live our lives allowing outside influences to control us, are we in the end much better off? It seems to me that if we don't take care, we can create our own concentration camp with the result that we may die before we have ever really lived.

So why don't we always make conscious choices that will lead to happiness and fulfillment? I've mentioned ignorance, and apathy, and laziness, but maybe there is an even deeper cause. Could it be that we simply don't believe in ourselves enough? Do we feel that we just don't have what it takes? Don't let this lid be a part of your reality. Choose as if you have it all.

I believe that negative choices, which sometimes may be the result of an unconscious decision to drift, can significantly affect the length and quality of life. You are put here to live, not merely to exist. But in order to do so you must take control. You must be in charge.

I may not have always taken control, but the majority of my life has been lived on purpose. I can tell you without hesitation that the positive choices I have made, whether they resulted in success or failure, accomplished one thing. They made me alive.

To choose for yourself is exciting, never boring. So my wish for you must be obvious. May you always take charge of your choices. In doing so you choose to really live. You have been given a gift. Accept it, use it, and enjoy the journey.

With Love, From Dad

2

Inspiration

"There is a deity within us who breathes that divine fire by which we are animated."

— Ovid - Roman Poet

Inspiration

Have you ever been inspired by music, a painting, or a stage performance? Most of us have. At various times I have been inspired to: 1) become an entertainer, 2) become an accomplished guitarist, 3) paint a sunset, 4) create a bronze sculpture, 5) become a better golfer, 6) take voice lessons, 7) improve my tennis game, 8) get in better physical shape, 9) put together a new seminar, 10) make more money, etc, etc.

I have acted on many of my inspirations, but usually not for long enough to do much good. Sound familiar?

So why don't we get inspired and stay inspired all the time? Would I ever like to have the answer to that one. Could it be that we are constantly seeking inspiration from outside ourselves? Could it be that we are waiting to be inspired?

The inspiration we receive from others is invaluable in our search to become the most we can become. However, the only lasting inspiration must come from within. When we are inspired, regardless of outside influences — that is when we take the wheel in our own hands and direct our own course; that is when we accomplish.

We should never stop seeking inspiration from outside sources, especially if it can keep us on track with the inspiration we have generated on our own.

Remember the last time you attended a meeting that featured a good motivational speaker and you came away with renewed resolution?

And just how long did that inspiration last? Maybe three days?

Without fuel from your own inner source of inspiration, outside influences fade quickly.

How do we get inspired in the first place? First we must have direction in which to aim. Then the most important ingredient of all must be added: action. Most of us wait to be inspired before we take action. Don't wait. Act and inspiration will give you wings to fly high. As the saying goes, "Perspiration precedes inspiration." If you will act "as if" you are inspired, inspiration will follow. Act enthusiastic and you will become enthusiastic.

Books and tapes can create a tremendous support system for your inspiration, but you are the key. The real maintenance of your inspiration will come from you. It is an inside job. Your thoughts are the controlling force. And you can control your thoughts. It will take effort. It may take affirmations, prayer, meditation or a combination of helping aids. Sometimes it doesn't take effort to get inspired. It does take effort to stay inspired.

Most people really love the feeling of being inspired. All kinds of good intentions are born. Accomplishment, however, will come when we stay inspired. Inspiration opens up our creative self to all kinds of possibilities. It is those possibilities that make life so beautiful. Life is being lived to its fullest when you are pursuing your inspirations.

I suspect that inspiration is God's way of urging us towards our true potential. Seems like we should take advantage of this blessing. So get on a roll. Let inspiration create action and action create inspiration. Become your own perpetual inspiration machine. What a great way to grow.

With Love, From Dad

3

Discipline

"He who gains a victory over other men is strong, but he who gains a victory over himself is all powerful."

— Lao-tzu

Discipline

Most of us exercise a lack of discipline in our lives on a fairly regular basis. Sometimes it is the inability to stay organized, to stay away from unhealthy foods, to work out regularly, to write home, or to be patient — the list can go on and on. So what I would like to discuss is why we lack that discipline when we know it will benefit us.

First of all, discipline sounds a little ominous. At least to me it doesn't "feel" like a positive word. In fact, it sounds like downright drudgery. If I have to discipline myself to accomplish a certain task, it smacks of using force or willpower. Have you ever heard someone say, "I just don't have enough will power"? The reference may be to a diet or an unpleasant task, never to an idea that involves fun. Can you imagine a person who loves to fish saying: "I just don't have enough discipline to go fishing"? No. Discipline is always applied in an area in which we struggle. If we like to do something, it doesn't require discipline. If we don't like to do something — well, you know the answer to that.

The question then becomes, "How do I discipline myself to do those things I decide I need to do?" Let me start by giving you something that won't work on a long term basis and that is willpower alone.

The energy behind the initial determination of those who have decided to lose weight, again and again and again, could probably fuel our country for hundreds of years. Unfortunately, most people just do not have enough pure willpower or discipline to stay with their commitment.

Does this mean they are weak? I hardly think so. I believe that they merely have used the wrong resource, teeth gritting determination, in striving for their goal.

Most of us lack the energy to use willpower alone to motivate us to our goals. We can be strong for a time, but eventually we fade and slip back to the path of least resistance. Our commitment loses power as time goes on.

The reason behind our failure to stay disciplined lies in the fact that our left "willpower" brain is in direct conflict with our right "imagery" brain. In other words, our left brain words are in conflict with our right brain pictures. Let me put it in the form of a quote by Emil Coué, the French pharmacist who, a hundred years ago developed a clinic where people healed themselves by the words and pictures they used. He said, "When the will and the imagination are in conflict, the imagination always wins."

Another quote, by an author unknown to me, says, "When your behavior gets ahead of your picture, you will always return to your picture." All this means is that no matter what you decide to change, if you try to do it by willpower alone, you are setting yourself up for a big fall.

So how do you go about successfully disciplining yourself to accomplish a chosen goal? Well, first of all you must learn how to change the picture you have of yourself in the area you desire to change. Unfortunately, this also requires some willpower and there is risk that the willpower will run out before the picture gets changed. It is, however, a risk well worth taking.

It stands to reason that in order to experience successful results in any goal you must first change your picture of who you are. A person who decides to lose weight, but continues to hold a picture of himself as a person who weighs too much, will never win. The golfer who wants to be a 12 handicap, but sees himself as an 18, will continue to shoot in the 90's.

What it all boils down to is this: you don't need discipline to help you stay organized if you are the kind of person who is organized. If you are not organized and that is your desire, you do need discipline to spend the time visualizing your goals on a regular basis, using techniques that are readily available. That is the only way you will change your picture, and that is the only way I know of to insert a different picture than already exists. Just remember, it doesn't take discipline to stay organized, or to work out on a regular basis, or to be patient, if that is just the kind of person you are. And it sure doesn't take discipline to go fishing.

So what will you need discipline for? Well, for one thing, you need it to investigate what I have told you about willpower versus imagination. Then, you will need it to follow through on what you discover.

The bottom line is this. If you are to make advances towards being the kind of person you want to be, it will take a little "guts" — and a lot of imagination. Why not use a little discipline to develop a big imagination? You'll get the picture.

With Love, From Dad

4

Limiting Attitudes

"Every noble thought is at first impossible."

— Carlyle

Limiting Attitudes

For the past few hours I have been sitting here, in a motel room in Seattle, designing insurance presentations on my Macintosh computer. It occured to me that what I am doing for my young clients is something that no one else in the world can do exactly like I can. In fact, it is something that very few insurance sales people can do as well as I can — mainly because of experience.

This line of thought led me to others and eventually to the idea that through my experience as a public speaker and motivator, I might, if I stretched my imagination, become a nationally recognized motivator. My daydreaming expanded into grandiose accomplishments with appearances all over the world to cheering audiences. As I was mentally basking in this flight of fancy I began to hear myself talking about all the stumbling blocks to my becoming a great speaker. All of a sudden I was filled with self doubt.

Follow along with me as in only a few seconds I went from high to low. Here were my thoughts:

> You don't look like a famous person.
> You need professional training in order to be good enough.
> You sure haven't proved you have "national ability" so far.
> Why would people want to listen to you?
> Your thoughts are not original enough.
> You are not good looking enough.
> People will think you are too old. Look at the wrinkles in your face.
> What makes you think you are good enough?

Fortunately, I became aware of what I was doing to myself. With that kind of negative programming I bet I could do a pretty good job of eliminating a great future in anything. What a lid I was putting on myself.

I decided that the positive needed at least equal time, and I immediately started answering myself with thoughts like these:

> Who says you have to look just so to be a great speaker?
> Who says great speakers have more ability than I do?
> Anyway, I am good looking enough and I'm definitely not too old.
> I do have the ability to do what I want to do.
> Besides, the world can use someone with my talent.
> By golly, why not?
> Let's do it - let's take the first step.

As you can tell, I ended on a very positive note, but a more important lesson was that I exercised my power to dismiss limiting and self-defeating attitudes. By reversing my thinking process, I took the lid off. Whether I become a great speaker is really not the point. What is important is believing in the possibility.

And this is my message to you. Right now is a perfect time to accept that you really are good enough to do whatever you make up your mind to do. What your negative self thinks or even what others think has nothing at all to do with your ability. Unshakable confidence in yourself is all you need. That, and some great visualization of what might be. You are enough — and you can do it.

With love, From Dad

5

Self Esteem

"No one can make you feel inferior without your consent."

— Eleanor Roosevelt

Self Esteem

Self esteem is something we all have. High self esteem is something very few of us have and all of us need. People with low self esteem feel justified in their appraisal because the evidence is in — just look at how they have fouled up their lives, according to them.

Low self esteem is a third class ticket to a miserable life. People with this malady, which has epidemic proportions, are not living their lives with a sense of joy or with the heart of a child. Life for them is the pits most of the time.

I guess everyone has the right to think of themselves in any way they want. Unfortunately, those who don't hold themselves in high regard have a tendency to inflict their misery on others. Also unfortunately, those closest to them are the ones who suffer the most. Wife beating and child abuse are certainly not a practice of those who have a high regard for themselves, and certainly do nothing to raise the self esteem of the victim.

I have often asked people to write down the things they would most like to change about themselves if they could. Time and time again their cards read, "I would like to feel better about myself."

The lack of positive caring for self infects the majority of people in the world, and is the root of all major problems of society. People who love themselves do not take drugs, commit crimes, start wars, mistreat their children, or mistreat themselves. People who love themselves, and others, are rare!

The initial blame for lack of self esteem must fall on the parents who often transfer their own lack of self worth to their children. Other culprits may include teachers, a church, peers or social mores that make victims of people rather than fully functioning humans.

A well known psychologist and friend of mine once told me that he contemplated suicide when he was twelve years old because while singing in the choir at Christmas he became so moved that he cried. This created terrible emotional conflict, because he was raised in a strict southern family that taught him that boys don't cry. He believed this so literally that when he did cry over the beautiful music, he knew there was something wrong with him and considered ending his life. A sad commentary on misplaced parental influence.

In spite of what influences colored your early life, the final responsibility for your self esteem cannot rest with anyone except you. Each individual has the final word. It is your choice. You can go on forever carrying the garbage someone else unloaded on you or you can decide that you are worthy, lovable and O.K.

"Yes, but — how can I love myself when I know how rotten I really am?" All I can answer is that rotten is a choice. God really did care when he created you. He gave you free will and the power of choice. And if you decide that you are valuable, then guess what — you will begin to act and subsequently feel that way.

If you are going to base your self esteem on being perfect, you are going to have a problem. If you are going to base your self esteem on being human, then you are starting with the right premise. You will make mistakes, but they should never detract from your essential value. You are the genius of God. Never forget that.

So, if you live your life on the basis of whether or not you were perfect in the past, you will be disappointed. If you live your life on the basis of what you can become — Eureka.

Feeling good about yourself is not only okay — it is a must. Call it what you will - high self esteem, self like, self love - whatever. Your life is meant to be lived in the light of your own self respect. Today becomes the day you account for. If you foul it up, as you may at times, just start over again tomorrow. You'll be better and stronger, and you will be one step closer to being the spirit you really are.

And, when you feel you are really loving yourself — regardless, then you can give that love to others — regardless. And that is a mighty important premise for life.

With Love, From Dad

6

Risk

"*Far better it is to dare mighty things, to
win glorious triumphs,
even though checkered by failure, than to
take rank with those
poor spirits who neither enjoy much nor
suffer much, because
they live in the gray twilight that knows
not victory or defeat.*"

— Theodore Roosevelt

Risk

A willingness to really live involves a willingness to change. A willingness to change involves a willingness to risk. A simple truth: No risk — no change — no life.

There are two kinds of risk, mental and physical, and while this chapter is primarily concerned with the former, it has been said that physical risk, within reason, can contribute to your psychological health. For instance, the element of risk is always present, to some degree, in snow skiing, but the reduction of that risk by developing physical competence is a rewarding process. It's almost like a release from self imposed boundaries, creating an emotional rush.

The risk that most of us face, and hesitate to take, is the mental one. I believe the decision not to risk is tied directly to our self image. It is fragile and we just don't like putting our ego on the line. The risk of being embarrassed, or rejected, or even ridiculed is avoided at all cost.

Taking a painting class could require a great risk for someone who has always maintained that he couldn't even draw a straight line. The risk here isn't that the person may find out he has always been right about his inability to paint. The real risk, in his eyes, is that other people will discover that his talent is equal to his poor self image and wonder how anyone so impoverished of ability could be so foolish as to attempt painting.

Isn't it easier not to take the painting class? Of course. "No risk — no pain." Sadly though, no pain equals no gain. Even sadder, no risk in one area promotes no risk in other areas. Eventually, not risking leads to apathy and apathy leads to non-participation in life.

What is involved in risk? Why are we afraid of it? Are we afraid of getting hurt, losing money, looking like a fool, proving to ourselves that we were really no good in the first place, or, heaven forbid, once again being rejected? Probably all of the above. I think most of us would rather take a physical beating than be subjected to mental abuse.

I kept good records at one point of my career in the life insurance business. Over one extended period of time I made over

15,000 telephone and in person calls to prospects. I disliked making darn near every one of them. Why? Simply because I was fearful of being rejected, of having people slam down the phone, or cuss me out, or be just plain nasty. To the best of my memory, not one single person was even slightly rude to me. Of course I had lots of "no's," but none of them were as I had imagined.

Of course, my imagination might have been fueled by Bert Harger, an old time insurance salesman friend of mine. He knocked on a farm house door one day and had it answered by a farmer who started screaming, "Insurance man, insurance man," the moment Bert introduced himself. Bert didn't know what was going on until he saw another farmer coming around the corner of the house with a shotgun in his hands. That was enough of the insurance business for Bert that day. I think it would've been enough of the insurance business for me forever.

You would think I learned something from all those calls. And I did. I learned that I still don't like to pick up the phone and offer myself up for rejection. I will do almost anything to avoid that risk. When I do avoid it, I can guarantee you that I am not creating happiness. In fact I have created financial hardship many times in my life merely because I didn't want to risk. The fact is, though, that when I did put myself at risk, even if I failed, I was much happier and lived a much fuller and more successful life.

We all have almost unconscious ways of rationalizing the avoidance of risk. You should try to be aware of clues in your behavior that tell you you are resisting risk for this simple reason. The less you rationalize, the more you expose yourselves to risk, and the more you expose yourself to risk, the larger your capacity grows for success.

One of the clues that I evidenced was physical. Each evening, in the insurance business, when I thought of going back to the office after dinner to make cold telephone calls, I could swear I was getting the flu. I would literally feel sick to my stomach. The urge, night after night, was to stay home. However, lack of money is a relentless motivator and off to the office I would reluctantly go.

Once in the office I would put a mirror on my desk, smile into it, and start dialing. After the first telephone call, a miracle would happen. The "flu" would go away, and each succeeding call became easier. In other words, once I risked — I got on a roll, and while I would never go so far as to say I enjoyed making those calls, I can absolutely guarantee you that I enjoyed having made them. It made me feel great to have me win over me.

Any change you make in your life requires risk. Accept it as a condition of growth and you too will win over you, and, feel great for having done so.

To live you must risk!!

With Love, From Dad

7

Guilt

"Better it were that all the miseries which nature owns were ours at once than guilt."

— Shakespeare

Guilt

Guilt! What an insidious waste of energy. What a giant barricade to human potential. What a bummer!

I was raised during an era of religion when management by guilt was in. I was one of its victims. I'm told that most religions teach a gentler ideal today, based on the love of God, not the fear of damnation.

I was brought up Catholic and went to a Catholic school until the ninth grade. Can you imagine my struggles when I was taught that I was a sinner if I so much as thought a sinful thought? I was convinced by the time I reached my teens that I was going to hell unless I happened to die coming out of the confessional. My thoughts had condemned me, and I was miserable.

Many people still have lingering pangs of guilt because of what they were taught about venial and mortal sin. I can look back at what I considered sin to be when I was young and now laugh at what a lonely place that interpretation was going to make of heaven.

There are arguments that insist guilt feelings are necessary. Nothing could be further from the truth. I'm not talking about having a conscience. That is our guide to right and wrong. I'm talking about the feeling that labels you as unworthy. Feeling unworthy leads to feeling unloved, and I don't believe God ever intended us to feel unloved.

Consequently, I don't think God intended us to feel guilty, only responsible. Pretty tough to say, "Love thy neighbor as thyself," and then condone the biggest deterrent to self love — guilt.

I do believe you must take responsibility for your actions and you must make amends. But once an act is committed, right or wrong, it is done, and there is nothing you can do to change it.

In my seminars I taught a phrase, "Then is then and now is now." What is past is past, so let it go, and concentrate on doing something about the now. I learned this concept from Dr. Ed Timmons of Louisiana State University. When he first expressed this idea, it was like a light bulb had been turned on for me. I gained new perspective and killed old dragons.

Are the old days of fear and guilt motivation gone? I guess that depends on your perspective. When I have asked audiences if anyone carries guilt feelings, the general response seems to indicate: "What a silly question. Of course we feel guilt."

So what am I telling you? Simply this. I do not believe that guilt has any place in your life. You have acted less than you are capable of in the past, and you will again. That is the human factor. But recognize that for what it is — an opportunity to grow.

Striving to become all you can become is the path to spiritual development. Failing now and then does not make you guilty. It merely affirms you as a creation of God - a fallible human being.

If you will merely be aware when you are not the person you want to be, that you have the opportunity and the responsibility to improve, then you'll be on the right track.

The core of this entire message is that you are a beautiful creation. A unique soul. You are worthwhile now, always have been, and always will be. You were born to love, yourself and others. Guilt has no part in that plan for your life.

With Love, From Dad

8

Self-Talk

*"Whatever kind of word thou speakest,
the like shalt thou bear."*

— Greek Proverb

Self-Talk

Florence Scovel Shinn, in her book, *The Game of Life and How to Play it*, has a chapter called,"Your Word is Your Wand," suggesting that the words you say are your magic wand and whichever way you wave the wand will determine what you receive in life. I am in 100% agreement.

I am not sure exactly how much power words alone generate, although scientific research has shown that words can influence body chemistry. That fact alone should keep us alert as to what comes out of our mouth.

Self-talk, by the way, refers to that silent dialogue we carry on with ourselves all the time, but also refers to the words we say out loud.

As I understand it, the three ingredients of thought are words, imagination, and emotion, and one cannot occur without the other two getting involved. Since words trigger imagination and emotion, and the combination of these three controls the results we experience in life, you need to be aware of what you say.

We talk to ourselves at a rate of about 600 to 1,200 words a minute, much faster than a normal speaking speed. Much of the time, as you have no doubt noticed, this conversation happens by default rather than on purpose. In other words, we are carrying on a conversation that we are not consciously controlling. On the surface that may seem all right. However, researchers have determined that the majority of thoughts running through our minds are of a negative nature. I don't know why we were created with such a great ability to dwell on the negative, but, by consciously changing the messages we transmit to ourselves from negative to positive, we can change our lives.

Simply put, if the words you say to yourself are vital to your health, wealth and happiness, and I am convinced they are, you need to be aware of what you say!!

We as a society have become so used to complaining about everything from the weather to politics that it is almost second nature to say things like, "Thank God it's Friday," or, "It's going as good as can be expected for a Monday." These are killer phrases. They are negative, they limit us, and I feel are a forecaster of future situations.

Just for the record let me list a few more popular killer phrases:

> —I just don't have the energy to run to get in shape.
> —I can't help it, I'm just no good with numbers.
> —I can count on it, every Spring and Fall I get a cold.
> —I just can't remember names.
> —Standing up in front of a group terrifies me.
> —The only kind of luck I have is bad luck.
> —You just can't trust people these days.
> —Everything I eat turns to fat.
> —I just can't quit smoking.
> —Why would anyone listen to me?
> —I'm just a klutz.
> —Everything I touch turns bad.
> —With my luck, I'll be at the airport when my ship
>   comes in.

Just think about the killer phrases you use, especially the ones that you are not particularly aware of. Could they be predicting your future? Scary!

"Yeah," you might say, "but how can I lie to myself and tell myself things are okay when things really are going bad? How can I say I have talent when I know I don't?"

Look at it this way. You've been lying to yourself about your potential all of your life. So why not lie good lies instead of lies that will harm you? I believe that when you say, "Things are really going good," or, "I never get sick," you are not lying — you are just announcing the future. And if present words can affect your future, why not use the words that say what you want rather than what your negative thoughts suggest you're not worthy of?

The mastery of positive self-talk requires the discipline to be aware of what you are saying at all times. Is is possible? Absolutely. Is it easy? Absolutely not. But so what. Your life is too important to leave to chance. Predicting a good future and having it happen because you exercise the discipline to watch what you say is a lot better deal than predicting a bad future with negative self-talk.

If I could give you a magic wand, which would be your

choice, a wand that worked good magic or a wand that worked bad magic? The choice of which magic wand is obvious. The choice of words is not so obvious.

But, your word *is* your wand. Use it for your wealth, health, and happiness. It really is worth the effort and you will be delighted with the results.

With Love, From Dad

9

Judging

"My soul, sit thou a patient looker-on;
judge not the play before the play is done;
her plot has many changes; everyday
speaks a new scene, the last act crowns
the play."

— Shakespeare

Judging

As I become more experienced in this life, I become more aware that to pass judgment is something that I am less and less qualified to do.

In my younger years it really did not occur to me to question my opinions. What I knew, I knew, and those who thought differently than me were wrong.

Today it is a constant struggle for me to be nonjudgmental, but at least I am aware that I need to watch my thoughts. I wish I could say that I am successful in this area of my being, but daily I find myself thinking that someone or something is wrong — according to me.

And isn't it easy for you, too, to assume the mantle of right? After all, what you know, you know, and those that think differently obviously don't know.

So let me ask you a question. Have you ever believed one way at one time in your life, and then believed completely differently at a later time? Of course you have. Santa Claus is a great example.

So why shouldn't we judge? Would it be an oversimplification to merely say, "Because we don't know?" Many things that we pass judgment on are really beyond our realm. I don't know to whom the quote, "Don't judge a man until you have walked a mile in his moccasins," is attributed, but it is a powerful statement of how we should behave. We rarely have all the facts to support our opinion. To judge one person bad and another good seems to me to be playing a role better left to a higher power, as Joaquin Miller so aptly wrote in *Byron*:

> "In men whom men condemn as ill
> I find so much of goodness still.
> In men whom men pronounce devine
> I find so much of sin and blot
> I do not dare to draw a line
> Between the two, where God has not."

What tragedy judging can bring. Six hundred thousand Americans died in the Civil War because of judgment on both sides that the other side was wrong. Hitler sent millions of Jews to their death because of his warped judgment.

I have heard it said that more people have been killed in the name of the Lord than in all the wars put together. Somebody besides the Lord must have been doing some judging. I wonder how God feels about that?

Of course, I have been talking about judging in the negative sense so far, but we can also commit errors of judging in the positive. I believe this story from the Chinese makes my point.

There once was a wise old Chinese man whose only horse was stolen from him. When the villagers lamented to him what bad fortune to lose his horse, he merely replied, "Maybe." A Chinese lord heard of his misfortune and gave him a fine horse. When the villagers remarked how fortunate he was, he merely replied, "Maybe." A short time later his only son fell off the horse and broke his leg, and the people said, "how bad," to which he replied, "Maybe." The next day the army came and conscripted all the able-bodied young men, but left the farmer's son because of his broken leg.

Each event was judged by the villagers to be good or bad, when in "The Big Picture" they had no idea if it was either. Isn't it the same for you and me? Don't we judge events based on our own perspective when we really don't know what the eventual outcome holds?

Tragedy and failure in our lives appear in the role of the bad guy, but how do we know they are bad? To paraphrase Earl Nightingale, "Out of every adversity there lies the seed of a bigger and greater success." I have lived much of these past years believing that with all my heart. No matter how great the tragedy, some lesson is there to be learned.

So my message to you is this. Stay aware that what or whom you are judging may not be as it or they appear. Beware of unbendable convictions. Be willing to learn, listen, and not to judge. Maybe this is not possible for human beings. However, if one of our tasks while in this dimension is to grow, then I think learning to withhold judgment is a great area to work on.

I will keep on trying to be open and nonjudgmental. I hope

you will also make the effort. When you try, you experience.
When you experience, and only when you experience, you have
the opportunity to gain wisdom, and when you gain wisdom,
maybe - just maybe- you will deign not to judge.

With Love, From Dad

10

Resentment

"How much more grievous are the consequences of anger than the causes of it."

— Marcus Aurelius

Resentment

Resentment is an awful disease. It is a form of mental cancer. It corrupts you with anger and makes you a "victim." Worst of all, it destroys joy in your world and inhibits your personal accomplishments.

I am going to ask you to play "pretend" for a few minutes and think in a novel way about how the negative power of resentment might affect your life.

I want you to pretend that you have just been told by an impeccable source that at birth you were given a measured supply of life energy, and that when you used it up you were finished here on earth. Would you be careful as to how you used your remaining energy? However, the rules of the game say that on any day you extend love, you will be given extra energy, and on any day you allow resentment to govern your acts, you will forfeit some of your energy. The purpose of this game is to arrive at an answer to this question: "Would you choose love or would you choose resentment?"

Silly game! But what if it were true? And maybe, in a manner of speaking, it is.

Carry this one step further and ask yourself if you would you ever give someone else the right to any part of your precious energy. I don't think you would, especially to someone who has wronged you. That is exactly what people do when they allow someone else to make them a victim.

They give someone else their energy.

In America we graduate 10 attorneys for every one that is graduated in Japan. In Japan ten engineers are graduated for every one that is graduated in the United States. Guess which country has a "resentment mentality?"

One country is productivity oriented and one is lawsuit oriented. "Sue the bastards" has become our national anthem. The energy from this kind of thinking is being directed 180 degrees in the wrong direction, and we are going to pay a price for it down the road.

Now that was a little like soap box oratory, but I think you understand what I mean. Please don't ever let "Sue the bastards" become your anthem even in the figurative sense. There is too much opportunity for happiness for you to indulge in the negativity of resentment.

Spending time resenting something, or someone, places the responsibility for your life on outside influences, and puts you out of control. Not only is resentment a waste of time, it is a waste of life. A lose/lose situation.

If someone wrongs you, feel sorry for them, not for yourself. Let them waste their life while you get on with the excitement and adventure that awaits you around the next corner.

And who knows, maybe, just maybe, you do have a quota of life energy that can be dissipated or replenished. One thing I can promise you: living life with healthy, loving thoughts gives you the chance for a long happy earth stay. Living with negativity makes for a short, miserable existence, though the days may number the same. Think about it!

With Love, From Dad

11

Regret

"For all the sad words of tongue or pen,
the saddest are these:
it might have been."

— John Greenleaf Whittier

Regret

Regret! What a waste of life's energy. Spending time on "what might have been," uses energy that could be spent on "what might be." And yet we are all guilty of wishing that some things might have been different. That is only human. It is dwelling on regret that immobilizes us for present action.

Everyone can point to events in his life he would like to change, but too much time spent in retrospect makes a person a victim of the past. When the "if only" syndrome becomes pervasive in a person's thinking, it has the effect of putting on the brakes and effectively paralyzing growth. That person goes on hold. Unfortunately, many people are on permanent hold and use excuses such as: "I'm too old," "Too late," "Too far behind."

Regret can furnish us with hundreds of reasons to abide in the past, reliving mistakes, wistful about missed chances, sad about things that might have been. Living with regret can cause feelings of inadequacy or ineptness and pave the road for excuses of poor performance.

Any time spent in the past, unless it is for reflection on what you have learned and how to do better the next time, can be relegated to useless daydreaming. And, when you are daydreaming negatively about the past and wallowing in the warm mud of regret, nothing gets done.

Past events fall into two categories: 1) Something you did or didn't do and can do something about, or 2) Something you did or didn't do and can do nothing about. That which you can do nothing about is not worth reconsidering except as a reminder not to repeat the mistake.

However, the first category is something you can do something about. I heard about a man who was bemoaning the fact that he hadn't gone to dental school when he was just out of college. He discovered that he could still be admitted to dental school, but argued that it was too late because, by the time he graduated in four years, he would be 44. His listener nodded and said, "Whether you go to dental school or not, one thing is for sure, you will still be 44 in four years."

When we experience regret, we are making an assumption that what we did or didn't do created a loss for us or someone else. We are judging that how things turned out was wrong. But that relates to the time and the circumstances. Let me illustrate:

My daughter Patti needed an ice making machine for her deli shop. She saw an ad in the paper for a brand new, but slightly damaged machine with an ice making capacity a little less than desired. The machine retailed for about $850 but Patti could pick it up for $350. Arrangements were made to look at the machine while she and I were on our way to the mountains for an outing. I was late and we missed connecting with the seller. Upset, Patti tried the rest of the day to make contact — to no avail. She was unable to reach him over the next few days and was convinced she had missed out on a great deal.

A few days later, Sam Philip, her father-in-law, found a used ice making machine with twice the ice-making capacity. The cost — seventy five dollars. Patti's regret flew out the window.

I believe we don't really know if an event we are experiencing is the best for us. Any time we spend "regretting" is a waste of time that could be better used to move forward.

If you have regret in your life and it is something you can do something about — do it. If you regret not having learned to play a musical instrument, start today with lessons. If you regret letting your body get in its present condition, start exercising and eating properly today. And be sure not to make the mistake of confusing what is possible and what is not possible. Some people will use age as an excuse, some will use lack of money, and some will use lack of time. But an excuse is an excuse is an excuse.

Do not limit your thinking. Use your imagination and make it happen. After all, Col. Sanders didn't even start Kentucky Fried Chicken until he reached retirement age. And Grandma Moses didn't start painting until she was in her 70's.

There is no room or time for regret in your life. It is never too late to right a perceived wrong. It is never too late to add action to your life. Regret is a rut, and a rut is a grave with different dimensions.

I urge you to use your time for being in the present and let the past be the past. Don't have anything to do with regret. Your whole life lies ahead of you, and you have today, and that is the only time that counts.

With Love, From Dad

12

Adversity/Tragedy

"If the world were a perfect place, where would souls go to school?"

— Emanuel's Book

Adversity/Tragedy

"I am an old man and have known a great many troubles, but most of them never happened." How nice of Mark Twain to set the tone for this chapter.

However, if a person lives long enough they are bound to encounter adversity and possibly tragedy. I've had my fair share of each. Each of us responds differently so I can only speak to my own reactions and perspective.

Because of my face to face duels with adversity, I have experienced anger, guilt, disillusionment, loss of faith, hurt, grief and eventually a small amount of insight. I have looked to the heavens and asked why and received no answers, but through the pain I grew a bit more, and, maybe, that was the good that came from the bad.

I have resolved that I must seek the positive side of any situation. But maybe there can be no positive that we can see for some adversity — it just appears to be a bad deal all the way around.

Death, unexpected or even expected, may seem to be the ultimate tragedy and yet I wonder at our assessment of that. The loss of Gary, our first born, has never completely left me — yet I have seen living, healthy children cause their parents much more grief than I suffered.

It seems so much easier to weigh the loss someone else sustains. Your perspective for them is somehow sharper than you can generate for yourself in a similar situation. Maybe an answer lies in developing the ability to step outside yourself when viewing a tragedy in your own life. That is easy to say and hard to do. Have you ever heard anyone say, "I understand that intellectually, but emotionally I am having a hard time dealing with it"?

I do know that time is a great healer, but also by stepping outside yourself you may be able to shorten the healing process. To say to yourself, "Life must go on," may seem cold and unemotional, but the simple truth is — "Life must go on."

Fortunately, most adversity does not take on the mantle of tragedy, but rather is just a difficult and somewhat unpleasant circumstance. That kind of adversity can well be handled by proper perspective. I am not sure that any time, without good perspective, is just exactly how you would like it. There always seems to be something that could be better.

I am reminded of people with whom I've skied in Sun Valley who complained about snow conditions, their adversity for the moment. But I can still remember many of those same times when I would stop on the hill, to catch my breath, and think, "All the money in the world can't buy this exhilarating, wonderful experience." Somehow, in spite of the snow conditions, I think my perspective gave me greater pleasure than theirs.

The truth is, most adversity is only adversity in your mind. And, you can control your mind. To judge a particular situation as adverse, without accepting that there may be a bigger picture, demonstrates a lack of understanding on our part. Things often happen to appear adverse which eventually prove to be for the best. Only time will tell. So give each adverse cloud its space. Then stop for a moment on the hill, step outside yourself, give thanks for the opportunity to grow, and get on with your life. The silver lining is waiting to shine through.

With Love, From Dad

13

Energy

"There is no genius in life like the genius of energy and activity."

— D. G. Mitchell

Energy

Energy is an attitude! If this raises a question mark for you, come play a game with me.

Let's pretend that it is Super Bowl time, you are a big fan of professional football, and your favorite team, the San Francisco Forty Niners, will be playing. Now here is the scenario:

You have just put in one of the most energy-draining weeks of your life, and today everything went wrong. You are so exhausted you are considering skipping dinner and just going to bed.

About 10 minutes after you get home, I call and say I am coming right over. I hang up before you can even reply. If the truth were known, you're sorry I called and wished I had picked another night.

When I arrive, absolutely bursting with energy, and say, "How long will it take you to get ready?" You are absolutely adamant, "No matter what you have in mind I'm doing nothing but being a couch potato tonight." But I say, "I just won a trip for two on a private jet to the Super Bowl, tickets on the 50 yard line, a hotel suite, all our meals are included, and we'll get a chance to go to the locker room and meet Joe Montana after the game. We have to be at the airport in 45 minutes, and it looks like we won't get much sleep tonight with all the pregame activities we are invited to.   Now how long will it take you to get ready?"

Well I guess you know the answer to that one. The truth now is that you suddenly aren't zapped, zonked, done in, spent, used up or even washed out. You have become a tornado in action. "Get out of my way. Super Bowl, here we come."

What has caused this transformation? The answer is that you've shifted your focus from mental distress and fatigue to a powerful idea that motivates you. Sure, this may be an extreme example, but it does prove a point. You have all kinds of energy just waiting to be called on. You simply have to refocus.

How do you do this? How do you keep yourself motivated enough so that you don't become "exhausted?" I believe the answer is a direct function of holding the kind of attitudes that do not allow for the kind of thinking that drains energy. Negative thoughts sap energy.

Positive thoughts stimulate energy. Allowing circumstance to dictate negative reaction is tiring and potentially health damaging at the best. Neutralizing negative input with positive output is a charge!

Of course there are physical reasons for not having energy, but most of the reasons are mental. The trick is in deciding which is which — and then doing something about the mental energy drainers.

Life is a lot more fun when you feel full of vim, vigor and vitality. It looks to me like the choice is yours.

With Love, From Dad

14

Givers and Takers

*"It is more blessed to give
than to receive."*

— Acts: XX, 35

Givers and Takers

When we are born into this world we are given a choice. Do we want to be guests of the universe or do we want to be givers to the universe? Unfortunately the fact that we have a choice is not immediately evident. In fact it may be years later that we discover there is a choice, and that we must make it.

I think that many people eventually come to a point when they feel the need to give meaning to their life. Sooner or later the question arises: "Why am I here? What is my purpose in life?" And last, but by no means least, "Why am I bored?" At this point we go out and buy books on mid-life crises. What we find out is that in order to get meaning we must first become a giver.

This creates a paradox because outward appearances indicate that in order to get what you want you have to take what you want. The truth is that the meaningful things in life are obtained by first giving.

At first glance, the takers may seem to have the best deal. They are like guests at a party. They appear on the scene, reach out for the food and drink that has been prepared for their pleasure and wait to be entertained. The hosts on the other hand have had their hands full taking care of all the details and then are constantly alert to the needs of the guests. When all is said and done, the guests go home, hopefully feeling that they have had a good time. But eventually, after so many parties, they may end up with a vague feeling of emptiness - another evening spent in meaningless conversation over too many cocktails. The hosts on the other hand, are exhausted, but in a good way. They feel, somehow, satisfied.

Scientists tell us that an absolute law of nature is the law of cause and effect. For every cause there is an effect. There are no exceptions. Let me ask you this: What is the difference between this law, and the Biblical law of give and receive? Are they not one and the same?

If you believe in the Bible and what it contains, you have to accept "give and receive" as a valid concept. If you don't believe in the Bible, then you are going to have to argue with a natural principle of the universe.

So if giving is a way to receive, why don't we do more than give lip service to the concept? I feel it is because we really don't believe that giving will work for us. It is valid for "them," but somehow not for us.

Maybe the problem is that we want results immediately. If we give to our spouse or friend, we want equal treatment immediately. If we give to the poor, we want tangible evidence returned on our so called generosity - now!

Nobody ever said, "Give to this particular source, and this particular source will give to you." The statement is, "Give and you shall receive." There is nothing mentioned as to what you will receive and where you will receive it from. This I believe - a life that dedicates itself to the practice of giving and receiving will not be missing fulfillment.

I really do not like categorizing people as winners or losers because I believe we all are born to be winners. However, when all is said and done, and life has been lived, the givers are the eventual winners and those who have persisted in a life of taking are the absolute losers.

I think you would be well advised to take inventory and see how you stand at this point in your life. Have you developed the host syndrome, or are you still being a guest? You have the choice.

When you make the decision to give of yourself, in whatever situation you may find yourself, you are guaranteed to come out a winner. By being unselfish you end up getting your "selfish self" satisfied. So the real paradox becomes: the most selfless thing you can do is the most selfish thing you can do.

Start giving with no strings attached and no expectations. You will be amazed at how much fun it is to be the host.

With Love, From Dad

15

Personality

"If you have anything really valuable to contribute to the world it will come through the expression of your own personality, that single spark of divinity that sets you off and makes you different from every other living creature."

— Bruce Barton

Personality

Personality is your flag, your coat of arms and your signal to the world of how far you have come in your quest for growth. Most of us fall into the category of most third world countries — underdeveloped.

This is so because we haven't defined who we are. We reflect a person who is confused and doesn't know his own truth. If the discovery of truth, our purpose in life, can be reduced to the simple serve, grow, and learn to love concept, then isn't the growth toward our best self, part of our discovery path?

And doesn't it involve learning to love ourselves and others? In growing and loving aren't we serving both ourselves and others?

More important than the external signs of a well developed personality is how having an advanced personality makes you feel. You should feel unique and irreplaceable. The full development of your personality will allow you to appreciate that fact and let it shine. You become a role model for yourself, and others will follow.

Your personality is a reflection of where you are on the growth scale. It is a state of being. If you don't feel good about yourself, your personality will reflect that. When you observe someone else acting out his beliefs through his personality, try to understand that that is just where he is at this present time in his evolutionary process. If some seem to be growing backwards, try to understand that too. Owning a personality trait of understanding is a great benchmark of your own progress.

There are many qualities to a fully developing personality. Here are six that merit your attention: enthusiasm, inquisitiveness, openness, patience, caring, and confidence.

Too many people subscribe to, "I am what I am," with no hope of change for future. It is O.K. to accept that your personality is what it is today. But remember, the fun in life is making it become what it can be tomorrow.

With Love, From Dad

16

Marriage

"Let there be spaces in your
togetherness,
And let the winds of the heavens dance
between you.
Love one another, but make not a bond
of living.
Let it rather be a moving sea between
the shores of your soul.
Fill each other's cup but drink not from
the same cup.
Give one another of your bread but eat
not from the same loaf.
Sing & dance together and be joyous,
but let each one of
you be alone.
Even as the strings of a lute are alone
though they quiver
with the same music."

— Kahlil Gibran

Marriage

Most believe in it. Most try it. Few succeed!

Most, if not all, marriages begin with a "Promise of forever," and a strong underlying physical motivation which starts out with, "I like the way you look — I like the way you act — and I sure would like to spend my life in bed with you." I realize that is an antiquated observation since marriage is not a prerequisite these days to spending a lot of time in bed with each other. However, I will not change my premise since sex is still a great motivator for the "Happily ever after" dream.

Unfortunately, hardly anyone is adequately prepared to build a true friendship, partnership, life long relationship. I suspect that anyone who does make it that far is blessed with an inordinate amount of luck and a great set of values. The bottom line is that we end up with a whole bunch of couples with a commitment to stay together in spite of a loss of physical and mental attraction, i.e., meaningless co-existence.

I may appear harsh in my assessment and even wrong, but I can count on one hand the truly loving, well adjusted, happily married couples among my friends and acquaintances.

What makes a good marriage? Well, the physical by itself just won't cut it. I read the other day that a good marriage can survive poor sex, but that good sex won't save a bad marriage. Sex is a part of a good marriage and only a part — and woe is the guy or gal that rates it number one. Of course, if all the other ingredients are rated A+ excellent, what great frosting on the cake.

Let's discuss some of the other ingredients that I believe are important for a happy lifetime together.

Observing happy couples that I have known, the number one ingredient most frequently is a solid spiritual base. Many of the other values seem to flow from this, such as kindness and empathy and attitudes of caring and giving.

I feel it is important to have common as well as separate interests. This might also involve quiet time together and quiet time alone.

Honesty is a given, as is a willingness to share inner

thoughts.   Patience is a major ingredient and requires the absence of imposed expectations on each other. It is important to realize that each partner is marching to a different drummer. This really requires deep understanding and acceptance.

Ever notice how some people lose the ability to have fun together? Fun is a biggie, and goes right along with laughing together. Show me a couple that laughs a lot — together and at each other — and I'll show you a marriage that will last.

Lastly, even though the list could go on, it would be really nice to have love involved. Not just love for each other, but love for self and love for others. That is the real frosting.

Is there such a thing as a perfect marriage? I don't know, but I do think that any couple that is aware of the above "ingredients" and makes an effort to include them in the relationship on a daily basis will have one heck of a great time together — for a lifetime.

With Love, From Dad

17

Trust

"I think we may trust a good deal more than we do. We may waive just so much care of ourselves as we honestly bestow elsewhere."

— Henry David Thoreau

Trust

It seems to me that so many people these days are afraid to put their trust in one another. I suppose this is because they have experienced hurt at the hands of someone they trusted and are not about to be hurt again. Do you sense a general attitude of, "You just can't trust people these days?"

It appears to me that to enter any kind of a relationship with an attitude of distrust has two immediate effects. Number one, the relationship, whatever its nature must be less than desired. And, number two, the person carrying the mistrust is bearing a seed of negativity that will grow and become the dominant factor in the relationship.

"Yeah, but what if I trust someone and I end up getting hurt?"

Baloney!! People with such an attitude are already hurting themselves and giving the other person no reason to be trustworthy.

I believe we do more damage to ourselves when we base any relationship on "half-trust" because we are setting ourselves up for a fall. We are actually creating the opportunity for harm to ourselves by anticipating what we have predicted. Then when the relationship changes, we affirm our negative stance by telling ourselves, "I knew it. I just knew they could not be trusted. Never again. People like that (or worse yet, all people) are just no good." And up goes the wall a little higher and down go our chances for a future relationship based on trust.

What if you carry the "heart of a child" attitude into a relationship (business, personal, sexual, financial, etc.) and you find out your trust is misplaced? Instead of saying, "Woe is me," why not let your heart feel sorry for the one who wasn't trustworthy? They are the ones with the problem.

And, just how badly have you really been hurt? Is it just your ego that is suffering? Did you lose money? Did a business deal go sour? Just what major impact will any of these have on the big picture, your life? Do you still have your health? Are there others who love you?

Things are hardly ever as bad as they may appear to be, and a much more life fulfilling experience can come from a temporary loss.

A good friend of mine was nearly destroyed by a divorce after 30 years of marriage. She had no skills for earning a livelihood, and no job experiences to draw on. A bleak and depressing outlook characterized her future until shortly thereafter she was introduced to a man who taught her to trust once again. She now knows a different and more exciting kind of happiness than ever before. A bleak dawn turning into a brilliant day.

So learn to trust, especially in the future and in yourself. It demonstrates a maturity, and a grace of understanding owned only by a few. May you be one of those.

With Love, From Dad

18

Integrity

*"Character is something each of us must
build for himself,
out of the laws of God and nature, the
examples of others,
and — most of all — out of the trials
and errors of daily life.
Character is the total of thousands of
small daily strivings
to live up to the best that is in us."*

— Lt. Gen. A. G. Trudeau

Integrity

"When the One Great Scorer comes to write against your name — He marks not that you won or lost — but how you played the game."

This sentiment was written by the great sportswriter, Grantland Rice, and seems especially appropriate to introduce the subject of integrity.

Can there be anything more important than integrity? It is the base of the soul — the "we" of who we really are. Our integrity furnishes us with the spiritual provenance from which we draw the inspiration for our dealings with others, and is the basis of our ability to be honest with ourselves.

Webster's Thesaurus uses the words "honesty" and "honor" to describe integrity. To that definition I would add, "Living up to the values we have established for ourselves." If my thoughts are accurate, then the judgment of others is not nearly so important as our judgment of ourselves.

I have tried new ventures at various times in my life, and these undertakings were not always perceived by a few as having integrity.

For instance, there was a time in the insurance business several years ago when, after considerable research, I spent more than $50,000 for a computer and software to be able to offer, what I considered, an exceptional service to my clients. It revolved around an idea that went against traditional thinking in the insurance industry, and I became somewhat suspect among some of my peers. It was very difficult for me to handle their rejection, but I maintained my position that I was acting in the best interests of my clients.

An interesting sidelight to the whole matter is that all of my peers in the insurance profession were, within the next five years, operating on a similar concept. So it turned out that my associates and I were the forerunners to an idea that the insurance industry itself eventually embraced. However, I found out that rocking the boat is not always the best way to make friends.

We have to live with ourselves. What allows us to do so with honor and peace is the foundation of our honesty — our integrity. I may have lost respect in the eyes of my insurance associates, but in my heart I felt I was right, and in the end that is what is important.

Some people believe that integrity depends on mutual agreement with a set of beliefs. "If you don't believe as I do and act as I do, then you do not have integrity." How many lambs have been led to slaughter with that kind of thinking?

So, the important theme of this message is that the integrity that really counts is the one you perceive in yourself. "To thine ownself be true."

Be honest with yourself. Do not participate in any activity in which you do not wholly approve. And that includes your inner thoughts. Do not participate in negative daydreaming. If certain thoughts do not meet your standards, eliminate them.

You have heard me say many times, "You cannot give what you do not have." You cannot give honesty if you do not own it for yourself. You cannot give honor if you do not have it yourself. You cannot give love if you do not love yourself. You cannot love yourself unless you are true to yourself.

And remember, the little things count too. If a clerk inadvertently gives you back too much change — return it. There is no such thing as almost honest. It isn't the clerk you are concerned with. It is you. If you compromise your integrity on minor matters, it becomes easier to compromise on bigger things, which compromises how you feel about yourself.

And — how you feel about yourself is the most important thing in the world.

So, take the responsibility for your own integrity. Live by your values. Doing so will empower you. Your integrity is the very essence of being.

With Love, From Dad

19

Be/Do/Have

*"If you would create something, you
must be something."*

— Goethe

Be/Do/Have

What a way we have brainwashed ourselves. Our lives seem to revolve around the idea that as soon as we have something, then and only then can we be or do something.

You have heard people say things like, "As soon as I have more money, I will be happy," or, "As soon as we have a house, then all our worries will be over." This kind of dialogue goes on all over the country twenty four hours a day. "As soon as I have, I will be."

How many examples can you think of where a wish has come true, but life goes on as before. This is because there is always something else to have.

It appears that constantly seeking to have something may be an indicator of what might be a global lifestyle. Our society appears to operate upon the premise that having something will allow us to be something. It almost seems that a typical life might evolve like this:

"As soon as I graduate from middle school and get in high school everything will be great. As soon as I make the varsity I will be happy. As soon as I can have a date with Sally — . As soon as I graduate from college — . As soon as I find the right job — . As soon as I get married — . As soon as, as soon as, as soon as."

And so we go through our entire life, seeking outside gratification from a source that is always just around the corner, only to find out that once we turn the corner we are simply faced with another corner.

A life of "have/be/do" is a life that is never truly gratified or fulfilled. So much of this kind of life is based upon material acquisition — a better car, a better home, nicer clothes, a vacation home, a boat, etc.

Isn't it amazing that once we get our new toy it isn't long before the newness wears off and we are ready for the next toy. I read a quote once that said, "The person who dies with the most toys — wins." Toy after toy, thing after thing, and what do we end up with? A win? Hardly. More like a vague, empty feeling that we have missed something along the way.

Have you ever known someone with more money than he or she can spend? I certainly have, and these people have never seemed to be the hallmark of a complete life. Howard Hughes comes to mind. What a miserable existence that rich (poor) man had.

So where does this all lead? To the idea that you must first "be" something in order to "do" something , in order to "have" something. Prove this to yourself by this simple experiment.

Take a blank piece of paper and divide it with your pencil into three vertical parts. Next, take no more than three minutes and list all the things you would like to "be" in the first column. Things, for example, like generous, patient, loving — whatever it is you want to be.

Once you have finished the first column, go to the second column and in the next three minutes, list all the things you would like to "do" in your life.

Finally, do the same in the last column for all the things you would like to "have."

When you have finished, look over your list and you will discover an amazing fact. All the things you want to "have" in your life are a direct result of the the things you want to "be" or "do."

If you want to have love, be loving. If you want to have enthusiasm, be enthusiastic. If you want fun in your life, be fun loving. If you want the heart of a child, be a child in your heart.

And if you want a life that returns full measure, then first give to life its full measure. You'll "BE" glad you did.

With Love, From Dad

20

Recreation

*"True enjoyment comes from activity of
the mind and exercise
of the body, the two are united."*

— Alexander Humboldt

Recreation

By definition, recreation means to create anew, to refresh, to restore. If we could spell it with a hyphen, "re-creation," it might have a more succinct meaning. Regardless, it is the catalyst for living a full life.

And, by recreating the fountain of your energy, you give yourself permission to function better at your chosen work.

Sometimes the work ethic that most of us grew up with nags us with guilt should we "steal" some time away. I discovered early on in my business life that my greatest periods of productivity were always accompanied by scheduled time for fun. So never feel guilty about taking time off for yourself. You are reinvesting in your personal success by stretching your body and mind and soul in some activity you really enjoy.

I had the opportunity to give talks in various parts of the country on how I used time management techniques to create success in the life insurance business. It must have made an impression because years later, people would come up to me and say they remembered me because I was the guy "who only worked three days a week."

At least they got part of the story. What I had told them was that I took every Friday, all day, to plan the next week. Then I followed that plan with intense focus on Monday, Tuesday, and Wednesday. For this effort I rewarded myself with Thursday, Saturday and Sunday off. A simple plan. One that was productive and profitable, and allowed me, for example, to snow ski every Thursday and Saturday for over ten winters.

I proved to myself that if you plan recreation into your life on a weekly basis, you create the opportunity to be even more successful at whatever you do. Maybe it causes you to work more effectively when you work in exchange for the right to play harder when you play.

There is another compelling reason, besides choice, for recreation. Our minds have difficulty being truly creative when engaged in the busy work of our job. Consequently we find ourselves falling into a rut that is short on growth and high on tedium. To be really productive, and creative, give yourself a gift of time, a chance to change gears. You'll discover energy you didn't know you had, and growth you didn't think was possible.

With Love, From Dad

21

Generosity

*"We must not only give what we have;
we must also give what we are."*

— Desiré Joseph Cardinal Mercier

Generosity

Have you ever wondered just what, "Generous to a fault," really means? Do you suppose it is really possible to be so generous that it would be perceived as a fault?

Generosity — how little there is in the place it belongs. When we speak of generosity we often think in terms of material or financial things, but I would like to speak to you about generosity as it applies to our inner spirit and our willingness to give of ourselves.

To be generous means to give. This starts with giving yourself the benefit of the doubt, giving yourself a pat on the back, giving yourself the right to be wrong, and most important, giving yourself love. You just can't go around liking yourself as long as you do good, and then disliking yourself when you don't meet your own, or someone else's, expectations.

It seems to me to follow that if you are not generous with your own expectations, that you will not be generous with someone you care for when they can't meet your expectations. And that is like saying: "If I don't deserve good treatment — then they don't either." Sooner or later one more relationship will bite the dust.

A generous person thinks of the good of the other person. A selfish person thinks of the good of himself. Now I don't suppose that comes as any great revelation to you, but I would like to offer the thought that the person who only thinks of himself or herself can never find happiness other than in little tiny bits of warped perspective. On the other hand, the generous person, is operating under the mantle of a widely accepted tenant, "As you give, so shall you receive," and will find happiness without seeking it.

It is impossible to give away something you don't have. So — if you have someone in your life that you really care about, or would like to care about (including yourself) then follow these two basic rules:

Rule #1 — Practice giving love, respect and patience to yourself.
Rule #2 — Practice giving of yourself.

The evidence is overwhelming. If you want to be unhappy
— be selfish.
If you want to be happy — be generous.
Wouldn't it be fun to be generous to a fault?

With Love, From Dad

22

Smiling

*"What sunshine is to flowers, smiles are
to humanity. They
are but trifles, to be sure, but, scattered
along life's pathway,
the good they do is inconceivable."*

— Joseph Addison

Smiling

I have been observing people's faces lately with an eye towards what they look like when they are not smiling, and what they look like when they smile. I believe people don't really realize what transformation takes place when they go from non-smiling to smiling. I am convinced that they don't realize, for that moment of smiling, they change their world. No matter what thoughts they were holding, all becomes light the moment they smile.

My favorite place to observe smiling is in the supermarket where everyone is preoccupied with what they are shopping for, and for the most part, not thinking awfully serious thoughts.

When someone comes my way I attempt to make eye contact. If successful, I smile at them and watch the results. Invariably I will get a smile back, and most times it is like witnessing a miracle.

I have seen ordinary faces turn beautiful right before my eyes — men and women. It is difficult for me to comprehend that the person returning my smile is the same person who was standing there the moment before. There appears to be a more significant transformation in women than in men, but, regardless, blank, weary faces turn into messengers of warmth. During that brief exchange of eye contact and smiling, people seem to radiate a flash of inner lightness. It is like that person is transformed from "non-living" into "living." The "birth of a spirit."

My "scientific" conclusion is this. At the moment of smiling the "subject" goes from a selfish entity to a selfless entity. A giver instead of a taker. And in doing so has experienced life at its best for a fraction of a second.

Now that may sound just a bit heavy to you, so I am going to ask you to try this same experiment. I know that going around smiling at strangers is frowned upon. After all, "What will they think?" Regardless, I would like you to see if you can experience the same "miracle" I have.

If smiling can produce an inner lightness, then my question to you is simply — "When was the last time you gave yourself a smile?" Try giving yourself an inward smile and observing the effect it has on your thoughts. Also, the physical act of smiling moves from the outside in, so get your face involved.

A favorite quote of mine is, "Life is too important to take seriously." I really believe this. I feel that most of us go around, most of the time, overconcerned about some facet of our life. Have you ever noticed that many people begin to develop "turn down" lines around the mouth as they grow older? Just as if they are in a permanently sour mood? Physiologists might contend this is just a natural sign of aging. I suspect it may be a natural result of less than positive thinking.

I would like you to try another experiment. Think of something negative that happened to you recently. Picture that event strongly in your mind — really reliving it. Now, smile while holding the thought. I believe you will find that you cannot honestly smile and still hold the negative picture. Doesn't this open up some possibilities for the next time a negative thought is occurring?

Smiling can offset negative thinking — and maybe some of its undesirable side effects. Make a habit out of smiling and you will be surprised at the changes that will happen in your life.

Also, how about getting your smile muscles involved the next time you are having an "important" conversation with yourself. Might change your perspective.

Try giving a smile to others when things are not going their best for you. The moment you give a smile and receive one in return — you will find relief from the seriousness of life. For that moment you will be living in the very present, and life, for a split second, will be great. If you can discover the secret of making life great for a split second, then don't you suppose it is possible to extend those seconds into minutes, and hours and days?

If you can prove this to yourself, then maybe you can convince someone else. Who knows where that could lead. Wouldn't a world of smiling, beautiful, warm-hearted people be absolutely tremendous?

How about you leading by example?

With Love — and a Smile, From Dad

23

Success

"Not in the clamor of the crowded street
Nor in the shouts and plaudits of the
throng
But in ourselves, are triumph and
defeat."

— Longfellow

Success

I read somewhere that, "If you can't do what you love, then love what you do." That would be just about as ideal an attitude as one could have. However, the latest estimate I read was that 97% of the people in America do not even enjoy, let alone love, what they do. Many of these are successful by the yardstick of material possessions. They have money, a big home, nice cars, fancy vacations and clogged arteries.

Unfortunately, success in life has become equated to money in the bank. Just as unfortunately, money in the bank does not necessarily have anything to do with happiness.

So, if money is not the hallmark of success, what is? I've given this question a great deal of thought and, of course, realize that we cannot abandon work to achieve happiness. In fact, fulfilling work can, and sometimes needs to, be the catalyst for happiness. It is just that I feel success cannot be measured in the traditional manner we are asked to apply as a standard of accomplishment.

Money is not the only consideration in our misdirected pursuit of happiness. The need for recognition has also been identified as a driving force. The acquisition of power is another one. But somehow, these, and others of a similar nature, come up short on the true success scale.

Success, as it is most commonly defined, is a false goal. If we pursue it in the traditional sense, I fear we may lose sight of what is most important. And this is the process of achieving personal grace — of becoming all we can become. This can only be accomplished in stages, as a journey is. Along the way we identify and pursue qualities that make the passage inspiring and worthy of the purpose of our being.

So if money won't do it, and recognition comes up empty, just what qualities of being do I feel are important for success? A partial list might look like this:

Good health and an awareness of what is good for you and what is not.

Peace of mind and appreciation for what is beautiful, the

sky, music, the laughter of children playing in the park.

Giving, whether it be in relationships or to help someone less fortunate.

Refusing to judge others who do not believe as you do.

Living, not for the moment that has passed nor for the one that is yet to be, but simply for the one that is.

Being kind to yourself even when you do not measure up to your own expectations.

Giving thanks for what you have.

Having dreams to pursue.

Creating action versus accepting inertia.

Acceptance of responsibility.

Laughter in the face of distress.

Graciousness in the face of adversity.

Viewing challenges as opportunities for growth.

Loving, yourself and others, without parameters.

Knowing that you do not know.

I hope you will take time to determine the qualities you want in your life that will be the yardstick you use to measure your success. Take those on my list that appeal to you and add to them as you go along the way. Then do your best to live by the standard you have set. It is the journey, not the destination, that determines your success. And who knows, with this perspective, you might even end up with money in the bank. I wouldn't be surprised.

With Love, From Dad

24

Quality of Life

*"Climb the mountains and get the good
tidings. Nature's peace will flow into
you as sunshine flows into trees.
The winds will blow their own
freshness into you, and
the storms their energy, while cares will
drop away from you like the leaves of
autumn."*

— John Muir

Quality of Life

Throughout this book there are a wide range of topics that can remain just that, or they can be integrated into your thinking and add to the quality of your life. It is that quality of life I wish to discuss with you in this chapter.

Earlier, I discussed living versus existing. Living life to its fullest does not necessarily mean living a long life. I believe it is possible to live a long life and never to have really lived at all. Quality and quantity are not necessarily roommates.

I recently read an article about an unusual human being named Ernie Davis, who was the recipient of college football's highest honor in 1961, The Heisman Trophy. Ernie was the first black man ever to be so honored. More important than his award, or his color, was the legacy of kindness, sportsmanship and loving that Ernie left when he died of leukemia at the age of 23. People are still influenced by Ernie, even after so many years, because of the quality of his short life. He was the kind of human being that, for whatever reason, seemed a step more evolved than the rest of us.

Quality of life is something that takes work. Your own life might be improved by the simple act of becoming aware of the qualities that you admire in others and would like to emulate, and then writing those qualities down as a reminder to yourself of what direction you want to go.

Here are some of the action principles I believe would serve you well in your pursuit of quality in your life:

- Love yourself
- Love others
- Give to yourself
- Give to others
- Serve
- Grow every day
- Refuse to worry
- Stay physically fit
- Read for motivation and inspiration
- Maintain positive self-talk

- Hold positive images
- Be creative
- Be thankful
- Eliminate resistance, regret and resentment
- Use your imagination
- Control your response to circumstances
- Exercise your power of choice
- Think happy
- Eliminate guilt
- Live for today
- Take time for yourself
- Be kind to yourself
- Be kind to others
- Have goals
- Forgive and forget
- Meditate or pray
- Keep perspective
- Eat for health
- Be enthusiastic
- Love life
- Be patient
- Eliminate anger
- Reject stress
- Encourage others to be all they can be
- Operate on purpose rather than by default
- Be aware that life is too important to take seriously

And remember, it is what you put into life that gives it value and meaning, both for you and for others who will gain from your example.

With Love, From Dad

25

Destiny

"Sow a thought, reap an act;
Sow an act, reap a habit;
Sow a habit, reap a character;
Sow a character, reap a destiny."

— Anon

Destiny

Do each of us have a destiny? Let me answer with a question. "Have each of us been born with special talents?" I believe each of us have talents that seem to come with the territory. I also believe that few of us ever get around to exercising those talents. So maybe we have all kinds of possibilities for a destiny. Regardless of the number of possibilities, I believe the responsibility for our future is up to us, and that our destiny will be a direct reflection of the degree of our participation in life.

If there is a preordained destiny, I believe it is to fulfill our talents. If that is so, I fear most of us will go to the grave with our destiny still begging. Maybe that would present a good case for reincarnation. We could just keep coming back until we got it right — kind of like being held back in the third grade.

Let me see if I can clear the air regarding destiny versus fate. Fate arouses images of out of control, helpless creatures who have been "predestined" to whatever. Destiny, on the other hand, communicates a possibility, a hope, a destination to be worked towards. "This is my fate," seems like a downer. "This is my destiny," seems like a light.

Maybe the talents you have been given are road maps to your destiny. If you are not pursuing your God-given talents, then perhaps you are drifting in a sea of fateful luck.

Even pursuing your talents may not bring happiness. Without perspective it may bring the opposite. Suppose you have acting talent and go on to be a great actor or actress. Would you be fulfilling your destiny? Possibly. Would this bring you the ultimate in happiness and joy? Maybe. Judy Garland, and Marilyn Monroe, and Elvis Presley seemed to be examples of those who were successful with their talent. Were they happy? Did they experience the peak of fulfillment? The way they left this world would suggest otherwise. They succeeded while failing. They completely lost their perspective.

Exercising your talents can be an unbelievably exciting and rewarding journey if you don't forget to exercise the talent God seems to rate right at the top — the talent to love yourself and others. If you exercise all your other talents, but leave this one out, success will be as nothing. Public acclaim will be meaningless and riches will be like ashes.

My definition of talent goes far beyond such skill as acting. A love of animals is a talent. It deals with your spirit. A desire to help the needy is a talent, a God given feeling. To be able to appreciate beauty is definitely a talent. Any intuitive feeling about what you feel you can do is an indicator of talent.

It seems to me that if there is a master plan, a destiny, for your life, it is to take what you have been given, and build on it forever with a base of appreciation for your intrinsic self worth as a unique human being.

This seems pretty basic when you think of it. Putting it into practice is an entirely different matter. But to follow your destiny is to follow what you were meant to be, and that is an absolute necessity if you are to gain all you can from your earth experience. It will take effort, and risk, and most likely rejection. Will it be worth it? As a friend of mine would say, "Absolutely, positively, totally."

Do I believe you have a special destiny awaiting you? With all my heart. You are one of a kind. You have a job to do in this life that no one else can do, a spot to fill that no one else can fill. May you always hold on to that belief.

In closing, let me leave you with my own version of a well known Irish blessing:

> "May your talents rise to meet you.
> May your light always shine from within.
> May the winds of love fill the sails of your spirit
> And may health, wealth and happiness
> be your destiny."

With Love, From Dad

26

Imagination

*"Imagination is the eye of
the soul."*

— Joubert

Imagination

Today is the 4th of July. What an appropriate day, Freedom Day, to write about the ultimate idea that will free your spirit — imagination. The only difference between personal freedom and bondage is how you use your imagination.

Napoleon said, "Imagination rules the world." Einstein insisted that, "Imagination is the world." He also said, "Imagination is more important than knowledge." If imagination is so important, why don't we use it more? Why impose ceilings on our accomplishments by failing to involve imagination?

Imagination forms the world we live in. It allows us to create ideas and separates us from the beasts of the field. But creation can be negative and imagination can populate a mental world full of doubts, self recrimination and feeling of unworthiness. And what kind of world is that? Many, if not most, would probably say, "The real world" — thereby affirming the negative thinking of our society.

Imagination is most effective for us when we use it to create a world of growth and happiness. But it takes practice, a concerted effort, like taking time out for exercising, to set aside a period each day for imagining.

Unusual coincidences began to happen when we use our imagination for growth on a regular basis. Ideas start to manifest.

I used to say, "The harder I work the luckier I get," — a well known axiom. And it was true. When I used my imagination on a goal with enthusiasm and determination, things began to happen.

Of course, it is easier to float through life than to row. But when we float, the "no can do" imagination takes over — and tells us that rowing won't get us there.

The development of your imagination is a process that leads from the idea to the visualization of it in a perfect state. Picture what you want to accomplish as if it already exists. Get yourself and your senses subjectively involved hearing, smelling, touching. Put yourself in the picture. Then add a big dose of positive emotion about what you see. Next, make sure you repeat this activity over and over in your imagination on a daily basis. Sooner or later, amazing things will happen.

Remember, understanding your imagination, and accepting that it is important, is knowledge. Using it is wisdom. Go for the wisdom!!

With Love, From Dad

27

Perspective

*"Perspective is the turned down corner
of a page in the
book of life. Wisdom is knowing there is
much left to read."*

— Wm. L. O'Hearn — Great Irish Philosopher

Perspective

Perspective! What is it?

My definition is that your perspective is your way of viewing life based upon previous experiences - real or imagined.

Why is it important? No big deal. It merely establishes the quality of the life you are living and predicts the life you will have. Whew! I want some of that. The problem is that while everyone has perspective, many hold a perspective that is out of sync with a happy life.

Your perspective and my perspective, dealing with the same facts, may lead one of us to cry and one of us to laugh. If I was laughing and you were crying, I would feel that your reaction was not "in perspective" - or "lacks perspective." You, in turn, might think I was out of my mind.

Many (Most?) people do not have their thoughts "in perspective" and consequently go through life manufacturing dissatisfaction, anger or misery for themselves.

It is my impression that people who lack perspective are living from the outside in. To understand this, visualize a circle about the size of a fifty cent piece. In the center of this circle imagine another circle the size of a dime. The inner circle represents you, and the area surrounding the small circle represents your circumstances and your environment. Now, much of the circumstances and environment in your life are beyond your control. If you live your life from the outside in, allowing "things" and "others" to control you - you are out of control.

On the other hand, while you may not be able to control what is going on around you, you can control your reaction to it. And by doing so you are living your life from the inside out.

Outside in people are called victims. They lack perspective.

Inside out people are called winners. They have things in perspective.

A valid question might be, "How can I keep things in perspective when so many negative things are going on around me?"

First of all you must make a personal decision about what, or which, perspectives you want to own — both generally and specifically.

To do that you must examine your thinking and set goals. Without direction, you exist. With direction, you live.

People who start their day watching television news reports and end the day the same way, then complain and get angry over the content of the news have lost their perspective, if they ever had it.

Keeping things in perspective requires thought, direction, study, prayer and purpose — and it just "ain't easy." So many times in my life I have lacked perspective. Our first child, Gary, was born with "multiple anomalies." I was told there were only two other similar births reported in the world that year. I had no perspective. God received a lot of negative conversation from me.

I could understand why he would punish me — I carried 300 pounds of guilt, good Catholic boy that I was. "But how unfair to punish Gloria and her folks and my folks," I thought. When Gary died nine and one-half months later weighing his original six pounds — my lack of perspective had increased. This crushing experience caused a breach in my relationship with God that was to last for years. Eventually from this tragedy I did develop some wisdom and from this I gained some perspective. God, eventually, did give me the serenity to accept the things I could not change — most of the time. And when other tragedies happened later in life, my hard earned perspective did help me handle things differently.

I still struggle with many situations and expect that this struggle will always be a part of my life experience. But that is O.K. because my perspective now is that I will have continuing opportunity to grow.

I still don't know the "why" of Gary. And maybe there is no "why" — or maybe the lack of "why" was an important junction in my journey through life. I will never know for sure, but I do suspect it was part of my learning curve and possibly the beginning of my life-long search for increased spirituality.

Here are some perspectives I own that I would like to pass on to you:

We are all worthy and special in spite of past acts or future acts.

Learning to love yourself first and then giving that love to others is primary. You can't give what you don't have.

Each adversity or tragedy in life offers positive opportunities. We must stay aware of this and be ready to grow when challenge presents itself.

The more I know — the more I realize how little I know.

Today is all there is. Any time spent regretting the past or waiting for the future is present time lost.

Guilt has no place in our life. Responsibility and determination to do better — yes. Guilt no!

THEN IS THEN AND NOW IS NOW.

The struggle for "things" will not bring serenity or happiness. The struggle might — things won't.

To take from this life and not to give back is to not have lived at all.

We must read if we are to gain knowledge and we must act if we are to gain wisdom.

None of us lives up to our potential — but striving to do so gives meaning to our life.

No one can teach you perspective. Perspective comes from the wisdom which comes from your experiences. Learning to accept your experiences with an open heart and knowing you do not know will give you a significant head start in your journey.

Remember. Inside out not outside in.

With Love, From Dad

28

Life's Pleasures

"One touch of nature makes the whole world kin."

— Shakespeare

Life's Pleasures

There are so many things in life to be thankful for. And almost always they are the little things. All too often they are things we take for granted, a part of every day life, that come and go without much thought.

I would like to share with you a few of the things that have added to my life. My list is not intended to be conclusive, merely broad enough to give you an insight into some of the things that have given me some moments of pure pleasure. Being a Dad to great kids is not on the list because that is a major blessing. These are just the little pleasures. See how they sound to you.

- A beautiful sunset
- A trusting relationship
- A good play
- A fine book
- A sunny morning
- A warm bed
- Good food
- Friendship
- Laughter
- A job well done
- A heart that is happy
- The smell of the sea
- A fresh tomato
- The majesty of the mountains
- A stream in the forest
- Wildflowers in a mountain meadow
- A warm fire on a cold night
- The wind against my face
- Newly fallen snow
- A starlit night
- Cloud formations
- A work of art
- A clean garage
- Physical activity

- Love
- The sound of children playing
- Fresh fruit
- Chocolate chip cookies
- Teamwork
- A great golf shot
- Physical fitness
- The color of leaves in the fall
- Peace of mind
- Walking on the sea shore
- Music
- Good health
- Someone to share with
- Windswept trees
- A cold drink on a hot day
- Finding an arrowhead
- Seeing wildlife in the forest
- The touch of a hand
- A good entertainer
- New knowledge gained
- Camaraderie
- A smile from a stranger
- Skiing in fresh dry snow
- Sun Valley
- The crunch of snow underfoot on a clear, cold night
- A sun-heated water shower in the Eastern Oregon Desert
- Freedom
- Harmony
- The smell and look of a fresh cut lawn
- Ducks setting their wings to a call
- A Thursday afternoon golf game
- A mid-week ski day
- A new moon
- A full moon
- Leaving on vacation
- Vacation
- A clean car
- A hot shower

- Having exercised
- A new idea
- A walk in the mountains
- Learning a new skill
- A four day weekend
- A massage
- A letter from a friend
- Breakfast on a sun-warmed patio
- The sight of geese flying south for the winter
- Walking barefoot in the sand
- The smell of turkey cooking on Thanksgiving Day
- Singing and dancing to rock and roll
- Hot feet in a cold stream
- The quiet of the desert
- A coyote's howl on a clear night
- The roar of the ocean at night
- A great movie
- Being in love
- The smell of spring
- A warm day in early spring
- Inspiration
- A tennis game with friends
- Working towards goals
- Being on purpose

Do you get a feeling from my list just how fortunate I am? Why not start a list of your own. Then make sure you are taking the time to enjoy the things you have written down. As you can see, so much of my pleasure has been as a guest of nature. I hope you'll accept her invitation. A beautiful day at the ocean or in the mountains can put things in perspective and add a lot of joy to your life.

With Love, From Dad

29

Wisdom

"As for me, all I know is that I know nothing."

— Socrates

Wisdom

Wisdom! What a nice sound — easy to say, hard to come by. How do you obtain it?

Wisdom must come from a combination of study and experience, the more of both the better. Many college students begin to believe they have developed wisdom because of all the theory they have digested. What they may not realize is that there is a tremendous difference between knowledge gained and knowledge applied — and that only through knowledge applied can they gain wisdom. Studying a book on how to swim will not teach you how to swim. You must get in the water. Similarly, studying how to live will not teach you how to live. You must get out and participate.

So if reading, or studying, by itself won't give you wisdom, and if sometimes even experience might not result in wisdom gained, how in the world do you obtain it?

I think the answer lies, in part, by reflecting upon values that have served you in a consistently positive manner, then using those values as an example to yourself of how you will perform in the future.

My own personal definition of wisdom revolves around a developed philosophy of living. A philosophy that embraces the concept that to truly live you must learn to love and develop the attributes that go along with that. Attributes like patience, empathy, understanding, and acceptance.

To me, wisdom implies a deep understanding of the important issues of life. The understanding that we are here to serve, to grow, and to learn to love. I think it also implies acceptance that we all are really all right — that we are children of the Universe — that we are one with each other — and by believing in ourselves we demonstrate gratitude to our Creator.

Maybe wisdom is too intangible to describe with mere words, but what follows is a an abbreviated list of attitudes a person of wisdom might own:

- Patient in all situations
- Tolerant of fellow human beings

- Operates in a state of harmony regardless of circumstances
- Accepts responsibility for his or her own growth
- Understands that thoughts create one's own world
- Accepts that things are not necessarily as they are perceived
- Doesn't worry
- Loves one's self unconditionally
- Lets go of guilt
- Strives to give love unconditionally
- Pursues perfection as a way of life while accepting that attaining perfection may not be possible
- Forgives oneself and others
- Non-judgmental
- Lives each day for itself
- Appreciates the gift of life
- Accepts adversity as a natural process of growth

There is so much more to wisdom than I have touched upon, but I think you get the idea. So what is my wish for you?

May you continue to develop wisdom in dealing with our world, so that the acceptance of "what is" will give you peace of mind and a positive outlook for "what yet might be."

With Love , From Dad

30

From the Heart of a Child

"How beautiful is youth!
How bright it gleams
With its allusions, aspirations, and
dreams!
Book of beginnings, story without end,
Each maid a heroine, and each man a
friend."

— Longfellow

From the Heart of a Child

My perspective: If you want to be truly happy, you must view your world from the heart of a child.

Society's perspective: A demand that you must grow up and leave the toys of childhood behind you. While we may not specifically hear the following admonition, the message comes through loud and clear: "Leave your day-dreaming, your imagination, behind you and come to this mature, no-nonsense world of adults."

Essential to a childlike heart is free imagination. I wrote about this gift earlier, but it is worth a reminder that most adults do not use imagination properly. We are never taught to use it and as children are strongly encouraged, albeit by default, not to use it. Children with active imaginations are many times the very ones who have the most difficult time in our left brained school system. One day we woke up and seemed too old to build sand castles.

As an adult, who sooner or later will hopefully seek simplicity in life, you must take the time to use your imagination. Actually take time to think, to dream, to imagine what your life can be.

Next, you must learn to laugh. And just how, for crying out loud, can you do that? Start by not taking everything so seriously. Many things you have taken seriously in the past year are gone from your mind now. They have zero effect on your life today. Carefully choose those things you need to be concerned about. If a circumstance is not going to have a significant negative impact on your life in the future, let it go. Don't give it any of your valuable energy. You don't find children spending hours creating needless worries.

Discovering the heart of a child in yourself starts with tearing down all the fences, stockades, and defense mechanisms you have built up on your way to adulthood. That is no easy task because some of your fences are brick walls 14 feet high.

The first fence to be dismantled is called distrust. You know the complaint you hear from people when they insist, "You just can't trust anyone these days."

Imagine how you would feel if a six year-old child were to

utter those words. After a wave of heartfelt sadness, you would want to have a talk with her parents.

But, if an adult says the same thing, people nod their heads wisely and agree.

How can you trust anybody? First you must gain some perspective regarding the outcome of trusting another person. If your perspective is harm, fear of getting hurt by opening yourself, then naturally you will hesitate to trust. The consequence of that perspective is that you play the role of victim.

As a victim, or potential victim, you will always have problems.

But what if your perspective refuses to give permission to anyone to make you a victim? How could you get hurt?

A child's feelings can be hurt easily — but a child has so many interests that it isn't long before he is absorbed in something else.

A child isn't vindictive, grudge bearing, or bitter. They get hurt, yes, but they bounce back fast. A trait worth emulating.

It is important to develop an attitude that allows others to be whomever they are. If others do not perform as you hope they would, then feel sorry for them, not for you.

Here are some of the characteristics I feel the, "Heart of a Child," might have that would be good for you:

>Enthusiasm
>Energy
>Curiosity
>Excitement
>Imagination
>Trust
>Forgiveness
>Devotion

How many more can you add? Wouldn't it be great to claim all these qualities as your own? It would make you more childlike. It would add meaning to your life.

With Love, From Dad

31

A Wish List

"I wish for you all the joy you can wish."

— Shakespeare

A Wish List

May you always have excellent health and limitless energy to make your tasks seem light.

May you gain spiritual insight early to make the game of life somewhat understandable.

May you always have freedom from fear or want.

May you always be moved to bestow love on God's creatures, and with a smile start with yourself.

May you never get caught up in the headlong rush to go nowhere, but, rather, take time to create something that is especially yours.

May you recognize your God given talents and use them to the fullest.

May you be the truest of friends and be blessed with true friends in return.

May you have the opportunity to travel the world and see that people are really not different, but are only waiting for you to step forward with friendship.

May your mind always be open and your confidence unbridled.

May you smile at adversity, but show empathy for those that do not have your insight.

May you be free of judgment, understanding that we humans do not have the capacity to understand the greater scheme of things.

May your perspective be gained from the heart of a child.

May you always realize that failure is a hallmark of growth, and the only people who don't fail are the ones who never try.

May you keep your successes and failures in perspective — they are neither an affirmation or denial of your self worth.

May you always be free of resentment and regret, for these thieves of love deserve not a moment of your time.

May you always be generous to those with less, pleased for those with more, and thankful for what you have.

May you not take circumstances too seriously — they will pass and you will have grown.

May you continue to use your mind to expand your knowledge of yourself, and others, and apply wisdom gained to enhance the quality of your life.

May you have an unlimited reservoir of enthusiasm, for it is the spice of life, and will bring joy to you and those you touch.

May you experience passion in your soul. It is the fuel of creativity, the elixir of life, and the mother of great accomplishments.

May you maintain faith that there is purpose to your existence, and that as you grow, and serve, and learn to love, you give meaning to that purpose.

May you take the cards that are dealt you and play them for all they are worth.

With Love, From Dad

Conclusion

Come to the edge.
No, we will fall.

Come to the edge.
No, we will fall.

Come to the edge.

He pushed them,
and they flew.

— Guillaume Apollinaire

CONCLUSION

Now you know what I feel. It is yours to do with as you wish. Like most lessons, these are only as good as the action you give to them. I would much rather have you develop a perspective that is different than mine and act upon it than to agree with me and do nothing.

For those lessons that may hold meaning for you, I urge you to make the effort to integrate them into your belief system. How do you do that? By being aware of what you are thinking. None of these lessons will merge themselves into your own reality without awareness. You must begin to act as if you already possess the traits you are seeking. The "As If" principle is vital to any change.

You may decide to seek out a role model - a person owning a trait you would like to own - and emulate his or her actions. You'll have to use your imagination. You'll have to exercise your power to choose. You'll have to risk. You'll have to monitor your self talk. You'll have to use discipline. You'll have to change your image of yourself.

Sound like a big job? Not really. Not if you'll look at your goal with imagination rather than logic. Life is a game. It is a place to have fun. If you want to grow, get less serious. It is like any game. The more you practice the easier it gets. The practice is the journey. Your enjoyment needs to be in the present, with the trip rather than with the final destination. Maybe that is because there is no final destination in our growth while we are here on earth. You'll discover, if you haven't already, that the farther you go the farther you can see. That is what makes life so exciting. There will always be lessons to learn, more games to be played, more fun to be had.

As you continue your journey, I want to wish you the very best in your quest. There are going to be detours and roadblocks. These are necessary for growth and gained perspective. When adversity strikes, as it will, keep things in balance. Look for the lesson. Give thanks for the opportunity to grow. Celebrate the challenge. From fire the steel is forged.

Through the tough times and the good times and the so-so

times, realize that what you are experiencing is life. It will be different tomorrow, and different yet the day after that. Make that exciting. Be eager for what lies ahead. Stay childlike in your anticipation. It's a lot more fun than fretting and worrying.

And if you can do this, what will you have gained? A gift of untold value. A gift of simplicity. A gift of openness. A gift of happiness. All because you acted From the Heart of a Child.

With Love, From Dad

About the Author

Bill O'Hearn's career includes 38 years in the life insurance industry as agent, general agent, and president of a life insurance company. In 1980 he founded the Alpha Learning Institute for the purpose of delivering the message of human potential through seminars and lectures. Bill, a proud grandfather of five, resides in Oregon where he pursues life as a speaker, consultant, golfer, skier, and outdoor enthusiast.

From the Heart of a Child is his first book.

MORE
BILL O'HEARN
RESOURCES

ORDER FORM

	Price	Quantity	Total
Books			
From The Heart of A Child	11.95	_____	_____
Tapes			
Relaxation	6.95	_____	_____
Relaxation with Affirmations	6.95	_____	_____
Spread your wings and fly	6.95	_____	_____
Shipping and handling 1-2 books			2.00
each additional book			.75
each tape			.75
TOTAL ORDER		_____	_____

- -

_____
(Your name, please print)

_____
(Street Address)

_____   _____   _____
(City)   (State)   (Zip)

_____   _____
(Business Phone)   (Home Phone)

If paying with credit card, please complete information below

| |Visa| |MasterCard| |Discover Card

_____   _____   _____
Card #   Expiration Date   Your Signature

Return this order form with check or money order payable to:
Entheos Publishing Company
P.O. Box 970
Wilsonville, OR 97070

TO ORDER TODAY CALL
503-694-5800 or 1-800-537-9991